DANA FOWLER

Mindfulness Skills for Adults with ADHD

Mastering Focus, Reducing Anxiety, and Enhancing Emotional Balance through Practical Techniques

Contents

1

Understanding ADHD and Mindfulness

1.1 Introduction to ADHD in Adults

Attention Deficit Hyperactivity Disorder (ADHD) is a neurodevelopmental disorder characterized by persistent patterns of inattention, hyperactivity, and impulsivity that significantly impact daily functioning. While it's often associated with children, ADHD can persist into adulthood, affecting various aspects of life, including work, relationships, and self-esteem.

In adults, ADHD symptoms may manifest differently than in children, leading to challenges in organization, time management, and maintaining focus. Adults with ADHD may struggle with impulsivity in decision-making and may find it difficult to sustain attention on tasks, leading to productivity issues and difficulty in completing tasks.

The diagnosis of ADHD in adults involves a comprehensive

assessment, considering symptoms, developmental history, and their impact on daily functioning. While there's no cure for ADHD, various treatment options, including medication, therapy, and lifestyle changes, can help manage symptoms and improve quality of life.

1.2 The Science of Mindfulness

Mindfulness is the practice of being present in the moment, fully engaged in one's thoughts, feelings, and sensations without judgment. Rooted in ancient meditation traditions, mindfulness has gained widespread recognition in recent years for its potential benefits in promoting mental well-being and reducing stress.

Scientific research has shown that mindfulness practices can lead to measurable changes in the brain, particularly in areas associated with attention, emotional regulation, and self-awareness. Studies have found that regular mindfulness meditation can increase gray matter density in brain regions involved in memory, learning, and executive function, which are often impaired in individuals with ADHD.

One of the key components of mindfulness is focused attention on the breath or bodily sensations, which helps anchor the mind to the present moment and cultivate awareness of one's thoughts and emotions. Through mindfulness practice, individuals learn to observe their thoughts without getting caught up in them, leading to greater emotional resilience and cognitive flexibility.

1.3 ADHD and Mindfulness: Finding the Connection

The intersection between ADHD and mindfulness lies in their shared focus on attention and self-regulation. Individuals with ADHD often struggle with regulating their attention and impulses, leading to difficulties in managing their thoughts and emotions. Mindfulness practices offer tools and techniques to strengthen attentional control and cultivate self-awareness, which can help mitigate some of the challenges associated with ADHD.

For adults with ADHD, mindfulness can provide a valuable framework for understanding and managing their symptoms. By learning to observe their thoughts and emotions with curiosity and non-judgment, individuals can develop greater insight into their cognitive patterns and emotional triggers, empowering them to respond more effectively to life's challenges.

Mindfulness practices can also enhance executive functioning skills, such as planning, organization, and impulse control, which are commonly impaired in individuals with ADHD. By incorporating mindfulness into daily routines, individuals can improve their ability to focus attention, regulate emotions, and make intentional choices, leading to greater overall well-being.

Furthermore, mindfulness can serve as a complementary approach to traditional ADHD treatments, such as medication and therapy. While medication can help alleviate symptoms, mindfulness offers a holistic approach to managing ADHD by addressing underlying patterns of thought and behavior. By cultivating mindfulness skills, individuals can develop a greater sense of agency and self-efficacy in managing their ADHD symptoms, leading to improved quality of life and overall functioning.

In summary, understanding the relationship between ADHD and mindfulness involves recognizing the shared emphasis on attention, self-regulation, and cognitive flexibility. By integrating mindfulness practices into their lives, adults with ADHD can develop valuable skills for managing their symptoms and enhancing their overall well-being.

2

Getting Started with Mindfulness Practice

In the journey of incorporating mindfulness into one's life, the beginning steps are crucial. Chapter 2 focuses on laying the foundation for mindfulness practice, offering guidance on creating the right environment, understanding the basics of mindfulness, and overcoming common challenges that may arise.

2.1 Setting the Stage: Creating a Mindful Environment

Creating a mindful environment is essential for fostering a conducive space for mindfulness practice. Here are some steps to consider:

- Choose a Quiet Space: Find a quiet and comfortable space where you can practice without distractions. This could be a corner of a room, a cozy nook, or even outdoors in nature if possible.

- Remove Distractions: Minimize external distractions by turning off electronic devices, closing doors, or using earplugs if needed. Creating a serene atmosphere helps to cultivate inner peace and focus.

- Set the Mood: Enhance the atmosphere with soft lighting, calming scents like lavender or incense, and soothing background music if it helps you relax. The aim is to create a tranquil environment that supports mindfulness practice.

- Use Props: Consider using props such as cushions, blankets, or a meditation bench to make sitting more comfortable. Proper posture is important for maintaining alertness and ease during meditation.

- Personalize Your Space: Make your mindfulness space your own by adding meaningful objects like candles, plants, or inspirational quotes. Having personal touches can make the space feel welcoming and conducive to practice.

By intentionally setting up a mindful environment, you create a sanctuary where you can retreat to connect with yourself and cultivate mindfulness.

2.2 Mindfulness Basics: Breathing and Body Awareness

Breathing and body awareness are fundamental aspects of mindfulness practice. They serve as anchors to the present moment and help cultivate a deeper connection with oneself. Here's how to get started:

- Focus on the Breath: Begin by sitting comfortably with your back straight and shoulders relaxed. Close your eyes if it feels comfortable, or soften your gaze. Bring your attention to your breath, noticing the sensation of the inhale and exhale. You can place one hand on your abdomen to feel the rise and fall with each breath.

- Practice Deep Breathing: Take slow, deep breaths, allowing your belly to expand on the inhale and contract on the exhale. Pay attention to the rhythm and pace of your breath, letting it flow naturally without forcing it.

- Body Scan Meditation: Shift your focus to different parts of your body, starting from the top of your head and gradually moving down to your toes. Notice any sensations, tension, or areas of discomfort without judgment. Simply observe and breathe into those areas, allowing them to soften and relax.

- Cultivate Present Moment Awareness: As thoughts or distractions arise, gently guide your attention back to your breath or body sensations. Practice non-judgmental awareness, accepting whatever arises in the present moment without trying to change it.

- Practice Regularly: Set aside dedicated time each day for mindfulness practice, even if it's just a few minutes. Consistency is key to building a strong foundation and deepening your mindfulness skills over time.

By cultivating awareness of the breath and body, you develop a greater sense of presence and inner peace, which can positively impact all aspects of your life.

2.3 Overcoming Common Challenges in Mindfulness Practice

While mindfulness practice offers numerous benefits, it's not uncommon to encounter challenges along the way. Here are some common obstacles and strategies for overcoming them:

- Restlessness or Impatience: If you find it difficult to sit still or quiet your mind, try incorporating movement into your practice. Walking meditation, yoga, or mindful movement exercises can help you stay present while engaging your body.

- Difficulty Concentrating: If you struggle to maintain focus during meditation, experiment with different techniques such as guided imagery, visualization, or mantra repetition. You can also try focusing on a specific object, like a candle flame or a sound, to anchor your attention.

- Resistance or Avoidance: If you resist or avoid practicing mindfulness due to discomfort or uncertainty, start small and gradually increase the duration or intensity of your practice. Remind yourself of the potential benefits and approach each practice session with an open mind and curiosity.

- Self-Criticism or Judgment: Be gentle and compassionate with yourself, especially when facing challenges in your practice. Remember that mindfulness is about accepting things as they are, including your own thoughts and feelings. Cultivate a mindset of self-compassion and kindness towards yourself.

- Inconsistency: If you struggle to maintain a regular practice, try integrating mindfulness into your daily routine by incorporating it into activities you already do, such as eating, showering, or commuting. Set realistic goals and prioritize self-care to ensure that mindfulness becomes a sustainable habit.

By acknowledging and addressing these common challenges, you can navigate your mindfulness practice with greater ease and resilience, ultimately reaping the benefits of improved well-being and inner peace.

In conclusion, Chapter 2 provides a solid foundation for embarking on the journey of mindfulness practice. By creating a mindful environment, mastering the basics of breathing and body awareness, and overcoming common challenges, you can cultivate a deeper sense of presence, awareness, and inner peace in your daily life. Remember that mindfulness is a skill that requires patience, practice, and self-compassion, and each step along the way contributes to your growth and transformation.

3

Building Awareness of Thoughts and Emotions

In the intricate landscape of mindfulness for adults grappling with ADHD, Chapter 3 emerges as a beacon of self-discovery and inner exploration. This chapter intricately unravels the threads of recognizing thought patterns, embracing emotions, and harnessing the power of mindful journaling as transformative tools in the pursuit of mindfulness.

3.1 Recognizing Thought Patterns in ADHD

The intricate dance of thoughts within the mind of an individual with ADHD often resembles a turbulent storm, unpredictable and overwhelming. Central to navigating this tempest is the art of recognizing thought patterns, a crucial first step towards taming the chaos and restoring a sense of equilibrium. Among the myriad thought patterns that individuals with ADHD grapple with, perhaps none is as both captivating and confounding as hyperfocus. This state of intense absorption can be a double-edged sword, fueling productivity and creativity while simultaneously trapping individuals in a vortex of single-mindedness. Yet, alongside hyperfocus, lies the constant companion of mind wandering, a phenomenon where thoughts flit from one topic to another with reckless abandon, leaving a trail of unfinished tasks and shattered focus in its wake.

To recognize these intricate patterns, individuals embark on a journey of introspection, turning their gaze inward with gentle curiosity and unwavering compassion. Mindfulness practices such as meditation and focused breathing serve as guiding lights, illuminating the labyrinth of the mind and offering glimpses of clarity amidst the chaos. By observing thoughts without judgment or attachment, individuals begin to unravel the intricate web of their inner world, identifying recurring patterns and gaining insight into the underlying triggers that propel them into states of hyperfocus or mind wandering. Through dedicated practice and unwavering perseverance, individuals learn to wield this newfound awareness as a beacon of guidance, redirecting their attention with grace and ease.

3.2 Embracing Emotions: Coping Strategies for Adults with ADHD

Emotions, like waves crashing upon the shore, ebb and flow with relentless intensity in the lives of individuals with ADHD. Learning to navigate this tumultuous sea requires courage, resilience, and above all, a willingness to embrace the full spectrum of human experience. Within the depths of emotional turmoil lies the transformative power of mindfulness-based emotion regulation, a beacon of hope amidst the storm. This practice invites individuals to bear witness to their emotions with unwavering acceptance, allowing them to rise and fall like gentle waves upon the shore.

At the heart of mindfulness-based emotion regulation lies the art of non-reactivity, a practice that invites individuals to observe emotions as they arise without succumbing to the impulse to react impulsively. By cultivating a spacious awareness of their emotional landscape, individuals learn to respond to life's challenges with grace and equanimity, rather than succumbing to the tide of impulsivity. Additionally, cognitive restructuring serves as a potent tool for untangling the web of negative thought patterns that often accompany emotional upheaval. Through the gentle practice of reframing, individuals learn to challenge ingrained beliefs and replace them with more balanced and realistic perspectives, fostering a sense of resilience and empowerment in the face of adversity.

Furthermore, seeking support from therapists or support groups can provide invaluable resources and coping strategies for navigating the turbulent waters of emotional dysregulation. Through the transformative power of therapy, individuals embark on a journey of self-discovery and healing, unraveling the knots of past trauma and learning to embrace the full spectrum of human emotion with unwavering compassion.

3.3 Mindful Journaling: Exploring Thoughts and Feelings

Journaling, like a trusted confidant, holds space for the whispers of the soul to be heard amidst the cacophony of daily life. In the realm of mindfulness, journaling emerges as a sacred practice, a gateway to self-discovery and inner exploration. Mindful journaling beckons individuals to set aside the distractions of the external world and turn their gaze inward, penning their thoughts and emotions with unwavering presence and intention.

To embark on a journey of mindful journaling is to embark on a journey of self-discovery and inner exploration. Each stroke of the pen becomes a brushstroke upon the canvas of the soul, revealing hidden truths and illuminating the path towards wholeness and healing. Within the pages of a journal lies the raw material of human experience, waiting to be transmuted into wisdom and insight through the alchemy of mindful awareness.

To begin the practice of mindful journaling, individuals carve out sacred space within the sanctuary of their daily lives, setting aside dedicated time each day to commune with the depths of their being. With pen in hand and heart wide open, they embark on a journey of self-discovery, pouring forth their thoughts and emotions with unwavering honesty and vulnerability. Through the gentle practice of reflection and introspection, they cultivate a deeper understanding of their inner landscape, gaining insight into the intricate web of thoughts, emotions, and sensations that shape their lived experience.

Furthermore, journaling serves as a potent tool for tracking progress and identifying patterns over time. By revisiting past entries with fresh eyes and an open heart, individuals gain clarity and perspective on the twists and turns of their inner journey, discerning recurring themes and uncovering hidden patterns that shape their lived experience. Through the gentle practice of mindful reflection, they cultivate a sense of self-awareness and empowerment, harnessing the transformative power of journaling to navigate the complexities of daily life with grace and ease.

In summary, Chapter 3 offers a rich tapestry of insight and wisdom, inviting individuals to embark on a journey of self-discovery and inner exploration. Through the transformative practices of recognizing thought patterns, embracing emotions, and engaging in mindful journaling, individuals cultivate a deeper understanding of their inner landscape, fostering resilience, and well-being on the path towards mindfulness.

4

Cultivating Focus and Attention

Attention deficit hyperactivity disorder (ADHD) is often characterized by difficulties in maintaining attention, which can significantly impact daily life activities such as work, study, and interpersonal relationships. In this chapter, we focus on various strategies and techniques aimed at cultivating focus and attention in adults with ADHD. From mindful attention training exercises to practical tips for improving concentration and adopting mindful work and study habits, this chapter provides a comprehensive guide to help individuals with ADHD enhance their ability to stay focused and attentive.

4.1 Mindful Attention Training Exercises

Mindful attention training exercises serve as a foundational practice for individuals with ADHD to develop their ability to sustain attention and increase present-moment awareness. These exercises involve training the mind to focus on a specific object or sensation while acknowledging and accepting distractions without judgment.

One effective exercise is mindfulness meditation, where individuals sit comfortably, focus on their breath, and observe the sensations associated with each inhalation and exhalation. When the mind wanders, as it inevitably does, practitioners gently redirect their attention back to the breath without self-criticism. Over time, this practice strengthens the neural circuits associated with attention regulation and promotes a greater sense of mental clarity and calm.

Another useful exercise is the body scan meditation, which involves systematically directing attention to different parts of the body, noticing any sensations or tensions present, and allowing them to release with each exhale. This practice enhances somatic awareness and helps individuals develop the skill of sustained attention to bodily sensations, which can be particularly beneficial for managing hyperactivity and impulsivity associated with ADHD.

Additionally, incorporating mindfulness into daily activities, such as mindful walking or eating, can further reinforce attentional skills by encouraging individuals to engage fully in the present moment experience without distraction. By practicing these attention training exercises regularly, individuals with ADHD can gradually enhance their ability to sustain focus and resist impulsivity in various situations.

4.2 Strategies for Improving Concentration

In addition to formal mindfulness practices, there are several strategies that adults with ADHD can employ to improve concentration in their daily lives.

Firstly, creating a conducive environment for focus is essential. This includes minimizing distractions, such as noise or clutter, and establishing a designated workspace that is organized and free from unnecessary stimuli. Using tools like noise-canceling headphones or white noise machines can also help reduce external distractions and promote concentration.

Breaking tasks into smaller, manageable segments can make them less overwhelming and easier to focus on. By setting specific goals and deadlines for each segment, individuals with ADHD can maintain a sense of progress and motivation, which are crucial for sustaining attention over time.

Furthermore, incorporating regular breaks into work or study sessions can prevent mental fatigue and improve overall productivity. The Pomodoro Technique, for example, involves working on a task for a set period, typically 25 minutes, followed by a short break. This structured approach can help individuals with ADHD maintain focus and avoid burnout.

Practicing mindfulness during task transitions can also support concentration by allowing individuals to reset their attention and approach each new task with greater clarity and intention. Taking a few deep breaths or briefly grounding oneself in the present moment before starting a new activity can help reduce distractions and enhance focus.

Additionally, incorporating physical activity into daily routines, such as short walks or stretching exercises, can improve overall cognitive function and attentional control. Regular exercise has been shown to increase levels of neurotransmitters like dopamine and norepinephrine, which play a crucial role in attention regulation and executive function.

4.3 Mindful Work and Study Habits for ADHD Adults

Adopting mindful work and study habits can significantly improve focus and attention in adults with ADHD. One effective strategy is to prioritize tasks based on importance and urgency, using techniques like the Eisenhower Matrix to categorize tasks into four quadrants: urgent and important, important but not urgent, urgent but not important, and neither urgent nor important. By focusing on tasks that align with long-term goals and values, individuals with ADHD can avoid getting caught up in distractions and maintain a sense of purpose and direction.

Breaking tasks into smaller, actionable steps can make them more manageable and increase the likelihood of completion. Using tools like task lists or project management apps can help individuals with ADHD stay organized and track their progress effectively. Additionally, setting realistic deadlines and holding oneself accountable can prevent procrastination and promote a sense of accomplishment.

Creating a structured routine and sticking to a consistent schedule can also support focus and attention by reducing decision fatigue and providing a sense of predictability. Establishing designated times for work, study, and leisure activities can help individuals with ADHD manage their time effectively and minimize distractions.

Moreover, incorporating mindfulness practices into daily routines, such as brief meditation breaks or mindful eating, can enhance overall well-being and cognitive function. By cultivating present-moment awareness and nonjudgmental acceptance, individuals with ADHD can develop greater resilience to distractions and improve their ability to sustain focus and attention over time.

In conclusion, cultivating focus and attention in adults with ADHD requires a multifaceted approach that combines mindfulness training, practical strategies, and consistent habits. By incorporating mindfulness into daily life activities, setting realistic goals, and creating a supportive environment for concentration, individuals with ADHD can enhance their attentional skills and achieve greater success in various aspects of their lives.

5

Managing Impulsivity and Hyperactivity

Impulsivity and hyperactivity are hallmark symptoms of Attention Deficit Hyperactivity Disorder (ADHD) that can significantly impact daily functioning and quality of life for adults with the condition. In this chapter, we will dive into understanding impulsivity and hyperactivity in the context of ADHD, explore mindfulness techniques for impulse control, and discuss the benefits of incorporating movement into mindfulness practice.

5.1 Understanding Impulsivity and Hyperactivity in ADHD

Impulsivity refers to the tendency to act without thinking about the consequences, often resulting in hasty decision-making and difficulty in inhibiting inappropriate behaviors. In individuals with ADHD, impulsivity can manifest in various ways, such as interrupting others, making impulsive purchases, or engaging in risky activities without considering the potential outcomes.

Hyperactivity, on the other hand, involves excessive physical movement and restlessness. Adults with ADHD may struggle with sitting still, frequently fidgeting or tapping their feet, and feeling an inner sense of restlessness. Hyperactivity can also manifest as an inability to engage in quiet, sedentary activities for an extended period.

Understanding these symptoms is crucial for adults with ADHD to effectively manage impulsivity and hyperactivity. By recognizing the triggers and patterns associated with these behaviors, individuals can develop strategies to mitigate their impact on daily functioning.

5.2 Mindfulness Techniques for Impulse Control

Mindfulness offers a powerful approach for managing impulsivity by promoting awareness of thoughts, emotions, and bodily sensations in the present moment. Through mindfulness practice, individuals with ADHD can learn to observe their impulses without immediately acting on them, thus gaining greater control over their behavior.

One mindfulness technique for impulse control is the "STOP" practice:

- Stop: When you notice an impulse arising, pause and take a moment to acknowledge it.
    - Take a breath: Inhale deeply and exhale slowly to center yourself and create space between the impulse and your response.
    - Observe: Notice the sensations, thoughts, and emotions

associated with the impulse without judgment.

- Proceed mindfully: After gaining clarity and perspective, choose a thoughtful and intentional response rather than reacting impulsively.

Another effective mindfulness technique is the "urge surfing" exercise:

- Sit comfortably and bring your attention to your breath.
- When you experience an impulse or urge, observe it with curiosity, noting its intensity and sensations.
- Imagine the urge as a wave in the ocean, rising and falling in intensity.
- Rather than trying to suppress or act on the urge, ride it out with mindful awareness until it naturally dissipates.

Regular mindfulness practice strengthens the prefrontal cortex, the part of the brain responsible for impulse control and executive functioning. Over time, individuals with ADHD can develop greater self-regulation and resilience in the face of impulsive tendencies.

5.3 Incorporating Movement into Mindfulness Practice

For individuals with ADHD who struggle with hyperactivity, incorporating movement into mindfulness practice can be particularly beneficial. Traditional mindfulness techniques such as seated meditation may feel challenging for those who find it difficult to sit still for extended periods.

Walking meditation is a mindfulness practice that involves

walking slowly and deliberately while maintaining awareness of each step and breath. This gentle movement can help individuals with ADHD channel their restless energy into a focused and mindful activity. As they walk, they can pay attention to the sensations of their feet touching the ground, the rhythm of their breath, and the sights and sounds around them.

Yoga is another excellent way to combine movement and mindfulness for ADHD management. Through a series of gentle, flowing movements and breathwork, individuals can cultivate greater body awareness, flexibility, and relaxation. Yoga poses can be modified to accommodate different fitness levels and physical abilities, making it accessible to individuals of all ages and backgrounds.

Incorporating movement into mindfulness practice not only addresses hyperactivity but also enhances overall well-being by promoting physical fitness and stress reduction. By engaging both the body and mind in mindful movement, individuals with ADHD can experience a deeper sense of calm and focus.

In conclusion, managing impulsivity and hyperactivity is a critical aspect of ADHD management for adults. By understanding the underlying mechanisms of these symptoms and integrating mindfulness techniques into daily life, individuals can cultivate greater self-awareness, impulse control, and inner peace. Whether through mindful breathing, urge surfing, or movement-based practices like walking meditation and yoga, there are various tools and strategies available to support individuals in their journey towards managing ADHD symptoms effectively.

Expanding on the topic of managing impulsivity and hyperactivity in adults with ADHD, it's essential to delve deeper into the nuanced nature of these symptoms and explore a wider range of mindfulness techniques and movement-based practices. Let's further examine the intricacies of impulse control and hyperactivity management, as well as additional strategies for integrating mindfulness into daily life.

Impulsivity and hyperactivity are multifaceted aspects of ADHD that can manifest in various contexts, including social interactions, work environments, and personal relationships. Understanding the specific triggers and patterns associated with these behaviors is crucial for developing targeted intervention strategies. For instance, impulsivity may arise in response to external stimuli or internal emotions, while hyperactivity can be exacerbated by sensory overload or boredom.

In addition to the "STOP" practice and urge surfing technique mentioned earlier, there are numerous mindfulness-based interventions that individuals with ADHD can incorporate into their daily routines. One such approach is mindful eating, which involves paying close attention to the sensory experience of eating, such as the taste, texture, and aroma of food. By slowing down and savoring each bite, individuals can develop greater awareness of hunger and fullness cues, reducing the likelihood of impulsive eating behaviors.

Mindful communication is another valuable skill for managing impulsivity in interpersonal interactions. By practicing active listening and nonjudgmental awareness during conversations, individuals can become more attuned to their own verbal impulses and the impact of their words on others. This can lead to more thoughtful and considerate communication, fostering healthier relationships and reducing conflict.

Furthermore, mindfulness techniques can be applied to the workplace to enhance productivity and decision-making. Mindful goal-setting involves clarifying priorities and breaking tasks down into manageable steps, reducing the overwhelm often associated with impulsivity and procrastination. Mindful time management techniques, such as the Pomodoro technique or time-blocking, can help individuals with ADHD stay focused and on track throughout the workday.

Incorporating movement into mindfulness practice offers a dynamic approach to managing hyperactivity and restlessness. Tai Chi, a gentle form of martial arts characterized by slow, flowing movements, can promote relaxation and body awareness while engaging the mind in focused attention. Similarly, Qi Gong combines breathwork, meditation, and gentle movements to balance energy flow and promote inner harmony.

Engaging in outdoor activities such as hiking, cycling, or gardening can also serve as mindful movement practices for individuals with ADHD. Spending time in nature not only provides a sensory-rich environment for grounding and relaxation but also offers opportunities for physical activity and exploration. By immersing themselves in the present moment and connecting with the natural world, individuals can experience a sense of calm and rejuvenation.

Moreover, mindfulness-based interventions can be integrated

into existing treatment approaches for ADHD, such as medication and psychotherapy. Mindfulness-based cognitive therapy (MBCT) combines elements of cognitive-behavioral therapy with mindfulness practices to help individuals develop a more adaptive response to their thoughts and emotions. By cultivating awareness and acceptance of their internal experiences, individuals can reduce impulsivity and reactivity while fostering greater emotional regulation and well-being.

In summary, managing impulsivity and hyperactivity in adults with ADHD requires a multifaceted approach that addresses the underlying cognitive, emotional, and behavioral aspects of these symptoms. By integrating mindfulness techniques and movement-based practices into daily life, individuals can develop greater self-awareness, impulse control, and overall quality of life. Whether through mindful communication, mindful eating, or mindful movement, there are countless opportunities for individuals with ADHD to cultivate greater presence and peace in their lives.

6

Mindfulness in Daily Activities

In this chapter, we explore how mindfulness can be integrated into daily activities for adults with ADHD, offering strategies and techniques to enhance awareness and presence in various aspects of life.

6.1 Eating Mindfully: Strategies for ADHD Adults

For individuals with ADHD, mealtimes can often be rushed or chaotic, leading to poor eating habits and potential health issues. Mindful eating offers a way to slow down and reconnect with the experience of nourishing the body, fostering a healthier relationship with food.

One key aspect of mindful eating is developing awareness of hunger and fullness cues. Many individuals with ADHD may struggle with impulse control, leading to overeating or ignoring natural hunger signals. By tuning into the body's cues and

27

practicing mindful awareness, individuals can learn to eat in alignment with their body's needs, promoting better overall health and well-being.

Another important aspect of mindful eating is savoring each bite. Instead of rushing through meals or mindlessly consuming food, individuals can take the time to appreciate the taste, texture, and aroma of each bite. By fully engaging the senses and paying attention to the experience of eating, individuals can derive greater satisfaction from their meals and cultivate a more mindful approach to nourishment.

Additionally, practicing mindfulness during meals involves bringing awareness to the process of eating without judgment. This means observing thoughts, feelings, and sensations that arise during meals without attaching labels or criticism. By fostering a non-judgmental attitude towards food and eating habits, individuals can develop a healthier relationship with food and reduce emotional eating behaviors.

6.2 Mindful Communication in Relationships

Effective communication is essential for building and maintaining healthy relationships, but it can be challenging for individuals with ADHD who may struggle with impulsivity and emotional regulation. Mindful communication offers a way to cultivate greater awareness, empathy, and presence in interactions with others.

One strategy for practicing mindful communication is active listening. This involves giving the speaker your full attention, maintaining eye contact, and showing empathy through non-verbal cues such as nodding and mirroring body language. By fully engaging in the conversation and being present with the speaker, individuals can improve their ability to connect with others and foster deeper relationships.

Another aspect of mindful communication is pausing before responding. Individuals with ADHD may be prone to blurting out thoughts impulsively or interrupting others during conversations. By taking a moment to pause and reflect before speaking, individuals can choose their words more intentionally and respond in a thoughtful and considerate manner.

Additionally, practicing mindfulness can help individuals become more aware of their emotional reactions during communication and respond with greater composure. By observing thoughts and emotions as they arise without getting swept away by them, individuals can cultivate a sense of inner calm and respond to others with kindness and understanding.

6.3 Bringing Mindfulness to Daily Routines

Incorporating mindfulness into daily routines can help individuals with ADHD cultivate a greater sense of presence, purpose, and intentionality in their lives. Rather than rushing through tasks on autopilot, mindfulness encourages individuals to engage fully in each moment and bring awareness to their daily activities.

One way to bring mindfulness to daily routines is to establish a morning ritual that sets the tone for the day ahead. This could involve practices such as meditation, journaling, or gentle stretching exercises to center oneself and cultivate a sense of calm and focus before beginning the day's activities.

Another strategy is to infuse mindfulness into everyday tasks such as showering, brushing teeth, or preparing meals. By paying attention to the sensations, movements, and actions involved in these activities, individuals can turn mundane tasks into opportunities for mindfulness practice and cultivate a greater sense of appreciation for the present moment.

Furthermore, incorporating mindfulness into evening routines can help individuals unwind and prepare for restful sleep. This could involve practices such as guided relaxation exercises, deep breathing techniques, or gentle yoga stretches to release tension and promote relaxation before bedtime.

By integrating mindfulness into daily routines, individuals with ADHD can cultivate a greater sense of presence, purpose, and well-being in their lives. Whether it's eating mindfully, communicating with greater empathy and compassion, or infusing everyday tasks with awareness and intentionality, mindfulness offers a powerful tool for managing ADHD symptoms and enhancing overall quality of life.

7

Stress Reduction and Relaxation Techniques

Stress is a pervasive issue for many adults with Attention Deficit Hyperactivity Disorder (ADHD). Its impact can exacerbate existing symptoms, making it crucial for individuals to develop effective stress reduction and relaxation techniques. In this chapter, we will explore the profound effects of stress on ADHD symptoms, delve into the principles of Mindfulness-Based Stress Reduction (MBSR) tailored for ADHD adults, and discuss various relaxation practices, including Progressive Muscle Relaxation (PMR) and other techniques.

7.1 The Impact of Stress on ADHD Symptoms

Stress is more than just a temporary feeling of pressure; it is a physiological response that activates the body's "fight or flight" mechanism. For individuals with ADHD, stress can magnify existing symptoms, making it harder to focus, regulate emotions, and manage impulsivity. The constant influx of stressors can lead to increased distractibility, restlessness, irritability, and difficulty in prioritizing tasks.

Furthermore, chronic stress can adversely affect brain function, particularly the prefrontal cortex, which is responsible for executive functions such as decision-making, impulse control, and working memory—areas already compromised in individuals with ADHD. This can create a vicious cycle where stress exacerbates ADHD symptoms, which in turn increases stress levels, creating a significant challenge in managing daily life and tasks effectively.

Recognizing the impact of stress on ADHD symptoms is the first step in implementing effective stress reduction strategies.

7.2 Mindfulness-Based Stress Reduction (MBSR) for ADHD Adults

Mindfulness-Based Stress Reduction (MBSR) is a widely recognized program developed by Jon Kabat-Zinn in the late 1970s to help individuals manage stress, pain, and illness through mindfulness meditation and awareness practices. Adaptations of MBSR for specific populations, including adults with ADHD, have shown promising results in reducing stress levels and improving overall well-being.

The core principles of MBSR involve cultivating non-judgmental awareness of present-moment experiences, including thoughts, emotions, bodily sensations, and the surrounding environment. Through mindfulness meditation practices such as focused attention on the breath, body scan, and mindful movement (e.g., yoga), individuals learn to observe their inner experiences with curiosity and acceptance, rather than reacting impulsively or getting caught up in negative thought patterns.

For adults with ADHD, MBSR offers several benefits:

1. Increased self-awareness: Mindfulness practices help individuals become more attuned to their thoughts, emotions, and bodily sensations, allowing them to recognize early signs of stress and intervene before it escalates.

2. Improved emotion regulation: By cultivating a non-reactive stance towards internal experiences, individuals with ADHD can learn to respond to challenging emotions with greater equanimity and self-compassion, reducing the impact of stress on mood fluctuations.

3. Enhanced attention and focus: Regular mindfulness practice has been shown to strengthen attentional control and cognitive flexibility, two areas of difficulty for individuals with ADHD. By training the mind to sustain focus on the present moment, MBSR can mitigate the distractibility and impulsivity associated with ADHD.

To integrate MBSR into daily life, individuals can start with short mindfulness exercises, gradually increasing the duration and complexity as they build their practice. Group-based MBSR programs led by qualified instructors offer structured guidance and support, providing a nurturing environment for individuals to develop mindfulness skills and connect with others facing similar challenges.

7.3 Progressive Muscle Relaxation and Other Relaxation Practices

In addition to mindfulness-based approaches, various relaxation techniques can help alleviate stress and promote relaxation in adults with ADHD. One such technique is Progressive Muscle Relaxation (PMR), developed by physician Edmund Jacobson in the 1920s.

PMR involves systematically tensing and relaxing different muscle groups in the body, promoting a deep sense of physical and mental relaxation. Here's a step-by-step guide to practicing PMR:

1. Find a quiet and comfortable space where you can lie down or sit in a relaxed position.
2. Start by taking a few slow, deep breaths, allowing your body to relax with each exhale.
3. Begin with your feet and toes, tensing the muscles as tightly as you can for 5-10 seconds, then slowly releasing the tension as you exhale.
4. Continue moving upward, progressively tensing and relaxing each muscle group, including the calves, thighs, buttocks, abdomen, chest, back, shoulders, arms, hands, neck, and face.
5. As you relax each muscle group, focus on the sensations of warmth and heaviness, allowing any residual tension to melt away.

6. Once you've completed the entire body scan, take a few moments to rest in a state of deep relaxation, savoring the feeling of calmness and peace.

Other relaxation practices that can complement PMR include deep breathing exercises, guided imagery, aromatherapy, and gentle stretching routines such as yoga or Tai Chi. Experiment with different techniques to find what works best for you, and incorporate them into your daily routine to promote stress relief and overall well-being.

In conclusion, stress reduction and relaxation techniques play a vital role in managing ADHD symptoms and improving quality of life for adults with ADHD. By incorporating mindfulness-based approaches like MBSR and relaxation practices such as PMR into their daily routine, individuals can cultivate greater resilience to stress, enhance self-regulation skills, and foster a sense of inner calm and balance amidst life's challenges.

8

Improving Self-Regulation Skills

Self-regulation is a fundamental aspect of managing ADHD symptoms effectively. In this chapter, we explore the challenges of self-regulation in the context of ADHD, explore the concept of mindful self-compassion, and discuss how mindfulness practices can help build resilience in individuals with ADHD.

8.1 Self-Regulation and ADHD: Understanding the Challenges

Individuals with ADHD often struggle with self-regulation, which encompasses the ability to control emotions, impulses, and behaviors in various situations. This difficulty in self-regulation can manifest in impulsive actions, emotional dysregulation, and challenges in maintaining focus and attention.

One of the core challenges faced by individuals with ADHD is executive dysfunction, which impairs the ability to plan, organize, and regulate behavior effectively. This executive dysfunction can lead to difficulties in inhibiting inappropriate responses, managing time effectively, and maintaining motivation over time.

Moreover, individuals with ADHD may experience heightened sensitivity to external stimuli, leading to sensory overload and difficulties in filtering out irrelevant information. This sensory overwhelm can further exacerbate challenges in self-regulation, as individuals struggle to focus amidst distractions.

Additionally, emotional dysregulation is common among individuals with ADHD, characterized by intense emotional reactions, mood swings, and difficulty in managing frustration and anger. These emotional fluctuations can interfere with daily functioning and interpersonal relationships, contributing to a sense of overwhelm and distress.

To address these challenges, it is essential to adopt strategies that promote self-awareness, emotional regulation, and impulse control. Mindfulness-based approaches offer promising techniques for enhancing self-regulation skills in individuals with ADHD.

8.2 Mindful Self-Compassion: Cultivating Kindness towards Yourself

Mindful self-compassion involves treating oneself with kindness and understanding, especially in moments of difficulty or distress. For individuals with ADHD, who may struggle with self-criticism and negative self-talk, cultivating self-compassion can be transformative in improving self-regulation and emotional well-being.

One of the key components of mindful self-compassion is mindfulness itself, which involves non-judgmental awareness of one's thoughts, emotions, and bodily sensations. By practicing mindfulness, individuals can develop greater self-awareness and acceptance of their internal experiences, reducing the tendency to react impulsively or harshly to perceived shortcomings.

In addition to mindfulness, self-compassion involves adopting a kind and supportive attitude towards oneself, similar to how one would treat a close friend facing challenges. This compassionate self-talk can counteract the inner critic common in ADHD, fostering a sense of inner warmth and encouragement.

Furthermore, self-compassion emphasizes the common humanity of human suffering, recognizing that everyone experiences difficulties and setbacks in life. By acknowledging shared struggles, individuals with ADHD can feel less isolated in their experiences, fostering a sense of connection and belonging.

Practicing self-compassion involves various techniques, such as self-soothing gestures, positive affirmations, and guided imagery. These practices can help individuals with ADHD develop resilience in the face of adversity, promoting a sense of inner strength and resourcefulness.

8.3 Building Resilience through Mindfulness Practice

Resilience refers to the ability to adapt and bounce back from challenges, setbacks, and stressors. In the context of ADHD, cultivating resilience is essential for navigating the ups and downs of daily life and maintaining a sense of well-being.

Mindfulness practices offer valuable tools for building resilience by enhancing self-awareness, emotional regulation, and coping skills. By developing a mindful approach to life, individuals with ADHD can cultivate greater flexibility, acceptance, and inner stability in the face of adversity.

One of the key aspects of resilience is the ability to regulate emotions effectively, especially during times of stress or uncertainty. Mindfulness techniques, such as deep breathing, body scan meditation, and loving-kindness meditation, can help individuals with ADHD regulate their emotional responses and cultivate a sense of calm amidst chaos.

Moreover, mindfulness fosters a mindset of curiosity and openness towards experiences, allowing individuals to approach challenges with greater flexibility and creativity. By reframing difficulties as opportunities for growth and learning, individuals with ADHD can cultivate a resilient mindset that enables them to thrive in the face of adversity.

Additionally, mindfulness practices promote self-compassion, which is essential for building resilience in individuals with ADHD. By treating oneself with kindness and understanding, even in moments of failure or setback, individuals can bounce back more quickly and effectively from challenges, fostering a sense of inner strength and confidence.

Furthermore, mindfulness encourages present-moment awareness, helping individuals with ADHD focus their attention on the here and now rather than getting caught up in worries about the future or regrets about the past. This ability to stay grounded in the present enhances resilience by enabling individuals to respond to challenges with clarity and purpose.

In summary, improving self-regulation skills in individuals with ADHD requires a multifaceted approach that incorporates mindfulness practices, mindful self-compassion, and resilience-building techniques. By cultivating greater self-awareness, emotional regulation, and inner strength, individuals with ADHD can navigate life's challenges more effectively and experience greater well-being and fulfillment.

9

Enhancing Executive Functioning

Executive functioning is a complex set of cognitive processes that enable individuals to plan, organize, prioritize, and execute tasks effectively. For adults with Attention-Deficit/Hyperactivity Disorder (ADHD), deficits in executive functioning can significantly impair their ability to manage daily responsibilities, leading to challenges in various aspects of life, including work, relationships, and academic pursuits. In this chapter, we explain the role of mindfulness in improving executive functioning skills for adults with ADHD, exploring its underlying mechanisms and practical applications.

9.1 Executive Functioning and ADHD: A Mindfulness Perspective

ADHD is characterized by difficulties in attention regulation, impulse control, and executive functioning. From a mindfulness perspective, these challenges can be understood as a lack of present-moment awareness and cognitive control. Mindfulness involves cultivating a non-judgmental awareness of one's thoughts, emotions, and bodily sensations, which can be particularly beneficial for individuals with ADHD.

By practicing mindfulness, individuals with ADHD can develop greater self-awareness, emotional regulation, and cognitive flexibility, all of which are essential components of executive functioning. Mindfulness meditation, in particular, has been shown to strengthen the prefrontal cortex, the brain region responsible for executive functions such as decision-making, planning, and impulse control. Through regular mindfulness practice, individuals can learn to observe their thoughts and emotions without becoming entangled in them, thus enhancing their ability to regulate attention and behavior.

9.2 Mindfulness Practices for Planning and Organization

Planning and organization are fundamental skills for effective executive functioning, yet they are often challenging for individuals with ADHD. Mindfulness practices can help improve these skills by promoting clarity of mind, reducing impulsivity, and enhancing cognitive flexibility.

One mindfulness practice that can aid in planning and organization is mindfulness-based cognitive therapy (MBCT). MBCT combines mindfulness meditation with cognitive restructuring techniques to help individuals identify and challenge unhelpful thinking patterns that contribute to difficulties in planning and organization. By cultivating a non-judgmental awareness of their thoughts and learning to reframe negative or self-critical thinking, individuals can develop more adaptive strategies for organizing tasks and setting goals.

Another useful mindfulness practice for enhancing planning and organization is the use of mindfulness journals or planners. These tools provide a structured framework for individuals to set intentions, track their progress, and reflect on their experiences in a mindful way. By regularly reviewing their goals and priorities with a sense of curiosity and openness, individuals can cultivate a greater sense of purpose and motivation, which can enhance their ability to plan and organize effectively.

9.3 Improving Time Management Skills through Mindfulness

Time management is a critical aspect of executive functioning that is often impaired in individuals with ADHD. Mindfulness can help improve time management skills by fostering greater awareness of how time is being spent and increasing the ability to prioritize tasks effectively.

One mindfulness practice for improving time management is mindful scheduling. This involves setting aside dedicated time each day for planning and organizing tasks in a mindful way. By taking a few moments to pause and reflect on upcoming deadlines, commitments, and priorities, individuals can create a realistic schedule that allows for breaks, self-care activities, and periods of focused work.

Mindful time tracking is another valuable technique for improving time management skills. This involves periodically checking in with oneself throughout the day to assess how time is being used. By noticing patterns of procrastination, distraction, or inefficiency, individuals can identify areas for improvement and make adjustments as needed. Additionally, by cultivating a non-judgmental awareness of their use of time, individuals can reduce feelings of guilt or self-criticism, which can interfere with effective time management.

In addition to these specific mindfulness practices, integrating mindfulness into daily routines can also help improve time management skills. By bringing mindful awareness to everyday activities such as eating, walking, or commuting, individuals can cultivate a greater sense of presence and focus, which can carry over into other areas of life, including work and productivity.

In conclusion, mindfulness can be a powerful tool for enhancing executive functioning skills for adults with ADHD. By promoting greater self-awareness, emotional regulation, and cognitive flexibility, mindfulness practices can help individuals with ADHD overcome challenges related to planning, organization, and time management. By incorporating mindfulness into daily routines and utilizing specific mindfulness techniques, individuals can cultivate a greater sense of purpose, clarity, and efficiency in their lives.

10

Mindfulness-Based Cognitive Therapy (MBCT)

Chapter 10 explains the application of Mindfulness-Based Cognitive Therapy (MBCT) specifically tailored for individuals with Attention Deficit Hyperactivity Disorder (ADHD). This chapter aims to provide an in-depth understanding of MBCT and its relevance in managing ADHD symptoms. It explores the core principles of MBCT, its integration with cognitive restructuring techniques, and the practical strategies for addressing ADHD challenges through MBCT.

10.1 Introduction to MBCT for ADHD

Mindfulness-Based Cognitive Therapy (MBCT) is an evidence-based approach that combines elements of cognitive therapy with mindfulness techniques. Originally developed to prevent relapse in individuals with recurrent depression, MBCT has shown promise in various mental health conditions, including

ADHD. The core premise of MBCT lies in cultivating mindfulness skills to become more aware of one's thoughts, emotions, and bodily sensations, thereby interrupting automatic patterns of negative thinking and reactivity.

In the context of ADHD, MBCT offers a unique perspective by addressing the underlying cognitive and emotional dysregulation that often accompanies the disorder. Individuals with ADHD commonly experience challenges such as impulsivity, distractibility, and difficulty in sustaining attention. MBCT equips them with practical tools to navigate these challenges more effectively by fostering greater self-awareness and self-regulation.

10.2 Mindfulness and Cognitive Restructuring

Central to MBCT is the integration of mindfulness practices with cognitive restructuring techniques. Cognitive restructuring involves identifying and challenging negative thought patterns or cognitive distortions that contribute to emotional distress. By examining the accuracy and validity of these thoughts, individuals can reframe them in a more balanced and realistic way, leading to a reduction in emotional reactivity and improved mood.

In the context of ADHD, cognitive restructuring addresses common cognitive distortions such as catastrophizing (assuming the worst-case scenario), personalization (attributing external events to oneself), and black-and-white thinking (seeing situations in extremes). Mindfulness serves as a foundational skill in this process, as it cultivates non-judgmental awareness of one's thoughts and helps individuals recognize the transient nature of their cognitive processes.

Practical steps in cognitive restructuring within MBCT include:

1. Identification of Cognitive Distortions: Individuals learn to identify common patterns of negative thinking that contribute to emotional distress. This involves observing the content and frequency of their thoughts, especially those related to ADHD symptoms and self-perception.

2. Challenging Negative Thoughts: Once identified, individuals are guided to question the accuracy and validity of their negative thoughts. They learn to examine evidence for and against these thoughts, considering alternative perspectives and interpretations.

3. Reframing Negative Thoughts: Through mindfulness practices, individuals develop the capacity to view their thoughts with greater objectivity and compassion. They learn to reframe negative thoughts in a more balanced and constructive manner, acknowledging both their strengths and limitations.

10.3 Applying MBCT Principles to ADHD Challenges

The principles of MBCT can be applied to address specific challenges commonly associated with ADHD. By integrating mindfulness with cognitive restructuring techniques, individuals develop a repertoire of strategies to manage ADHD symptoms more effectively and enhance overall well-being.

Some key areas where MBCT principles can be applied in the context of ADHD include:

1. Impulsivity Management: Mindfulness practices such as focused attention meditation help individuals cultivate greater impulse control by strengthening their ability to pause and respond thoughtfully rather than react impulsively. Cognitive restructuring techniques assist in challenging impulsive thoughts and considering the potential consequences of actions.

2. Attention Regulation: Mindfulness-based attention training exercises improve attentional focus and concentration by training individuals to sustain their awareness on a chosen object or anchor, such as the breath or bodily sensations. This enhances cognitive flexibility and resilience in the face of distractions, a common challenge for individuals with ADHD.

3. Emotional Regulation: By developing mindfulness skills, individuals with ADHD learn to observe their emotions with greater equanimity and acceptance, reducing emotional reactivity and impulsivity. Cognitive restructuring techniques help in reframing negative emotions and cultivating a more balanced perspective, leading to improved emotional regulation and resilience.

By combining mindfulness practices with cognitive restructuring techniques, individuals with ADHD can develop greater self-awareness, emotional regulation, and cognitive flexibility, leading to enhanced well-being and symptom management. Through practical exercises and strategies, MBCT empowers individuals to cultivate a more mindful approach to living with

ADHD, fostering resilience and adaptive coping skills.

11

Mindfulness in Coping with ADHD Symptoms

In the journey of managing Attention Deficit Hyperactivity Disorder (ADHD), individuals often encounter various challenges that extend beyond the core symptoms of impulsivity, inattention, and hyperactivity. Mood swings, rejection sensitivity, shame, guilt, and medication side effects are among the common hurdles that adults with ADHD face. Mindfulness, with its emphasis on present moment awareness and non-judgmental acceptance, offers valuable tools for coping with these challenges effectively.

11.1 Mindfulness for Managing Mood Swings and Rejection Sensitivity

Mood swings and heightened sensitivity to rejection are prevalent among individuals with ADHD. These fluctuations in mood and intense reactions to perceived rejection can significantly impact daily functioning and interpersonal relationships. Mindfulness-based interventions can be particularly beneficial in managing these symptoms by cultivating emotional regulation and resilience.

One mindfulness technique that can help manage mood swings is the practice of observing emotions without reacting to them. Through mindfulness meditation, individuals learn to become aware of their emotional states without automatically acting on them. By simply observing the emotions as they arise, individuals create a space between the emotion and their response, allowing for a more mindful and intentional reaction.

Additionally, mindfulness practices such as loving-kindness meditation can help individuals develop compassion towards themselves and others. By cultivating feelings of kindness and acceptance, individuals with ADHD can reduce self-criticism and improve their ability to handle rejection more gracefully. This practice involves silently repeating phrases of goodwill towards oneself and others, fostering a sense of interconnectedness and understanding.

Furthermore, mindfulness-based cognitive therapy (MBCT) techniques can be employed to challenge negative thought patterns associated with mood swings and rejection sensitivity. Through mindfulness, individuals learn to recognize and reframe negative thoughts, reducing their impact on emotional well-being. By practicing mindfulness regularly, individuals with ADHD can develop greater emotional resilience and a more balanced response to life's challenges.

11.2 Dealing with ADHD-related Shame and Guilt Mindfully

Shame and guilt are common experiences for individuals with ADHD, stemming from perceived failures, difficulties in meeting expectations, and societal stigma surrounding the disorder. These negative emotions can contribute to low self-esteem, depression, and avoidance behaviors. Mindfulness offers a compassionate approach to addressing shame and guilt by promoting self-acceptance and self-compassion.

Mindfulness practices such as body scan meditation can help individuals with ADHD develop greater awareness of bodily sensations associated with shame and guilt. By bringing attention to these sensations without judgment, individuals can begin to understand the physical manifestations of these emotions and their impact on overall well-being.

Self-compassion meditation is another powerful tool for dealing with shame and guilt mindfully. This practice involves extending kindness and understanding towards oneself in moments of difficulty or self-criticism. By recognizing one's common humanity and inherent worthiness, individuals with ADHD can cultivate a sense of self-compassion that counteracts feelings of shame and guilt.

Moreover, mindfulness-based approaches to shame and guilt often involve challenging negative self-beliefs through cognitive restructuring. By examining the evidence for and against these beliefs in a mindful and compassionate manner, individuals can begin to develop more balanced and realistic perspectives of themselves and their experiences.

11.3 Mindfulness for Coping with ADHD Medication Side Effects

While medication can be an effective treatment for managing ADHD symptoms, it often comes with side effects that can impact quality of life. Common side effects include insomnia, decreased appetite, irritability, and mood swings. Mindfulness techniques can be employed to cope with these side effects and enhance overall well-being.

Mindful awareness of physical sensations can help individuals with ADHD become more attuned to the subtle changes in their bodies associated with medication side effects. By paying attention to sensations such as tension, discomfort, or restlessness without judgment, individuals can develop greater self-awareness and agency in managing these symptoms.

Mindfulness-based stress reduction (MBSR) techniques, such as mindful breathing and body scanning, can help individuals with ADHD reduce stress and anxiety associated with medication side effects. By practicing these techniques regularly, individuals can cultivate a sense of calm and relaxation that counteracts the physiological arousal often experienced with stimulant medications.

Additionally, mindfulness can aid in managing emotional reactivity and impulsivity, which may be exacerbated by medication side effects. By cultivating present moment awareness and non-reactivity, individuals can develop greater emotional regulation and resilience in the face of challenging symptoms.

Furthermore, mindfulness practices such as mindful eating can support individuals in maintaining a healthy appetite and nutritional balance despite potential appetite suppression from medication. By bringing mindful awareness to the eating process, individuals can enhance their enjoyment of food and make conscious choices that support their overall well-being.

In summary, mindfulness skills offer valuable strategies for coping with the various challenges associated with ADHD, including mood swings, rejection sensitivity, shame, guilt, and medication side effects. By cultivating present moment awareness, self-compassion, and emotional regulation, individuals with ADHD can enhance their overall well-being and quality of life. Through regular mindfulness practice, individuals can develop resilience and empower themselves to navigate the complexities of living with ADHD with greater ease and grace.

12

Cultivating Gratitude and Positive Psychology

In the realm of ADHD management, cultivating gratitude and embracing positive psychology can serve as powerful tools for individuals navigating the challenges associated with attention deficit hyperactivity disorder (ADHD). This chapter delves into the transformative effects of gratitude practices, the efficacy of positive affirmations and mindful reflection, and the integration of mindfulness with principles of positive psychology to enhance well-being and resilience.

12.1 The Power of Gratitude in ADHD Management

Gratitude, often described as the practice of recognizing and appreciating the positive aspects of life, has garnered attention in recent years for its profound impact on mental health and overall well-being. For adults with ADHD, who may frequently encounter struggles and setbacks in their daily lives, incorporating gratitude into their routine can be particularly beneficial.

Research suggests that cultivating gratitude can lead to improvements in mood, resilience, and overall life satisfaction. By intentionally focusing on the blessings, no matter how small, individuals with ADHD can shift their perspective from one of scarcity to abundance. This shift in mindset can help counteract the negative thought patterns and emotional dysregulation often associated with ADHD.

Practical strategies for incorporating gratitude into daily life may include keeping a gratitude journal, where individuals can regularly reflect on and write down things they are thankful for. This simple yet powerful practice encourages mindfulness and fosters a sense of appreciation for the present moment. Additionally, expressing gratitude verbally or through acts of kindness towards others can further reinforce positive emotions and strengthen social connections, which are vital for emotional well-being.

12.2 Practicing Positive Affirmations and Mindful Reflection

Positive affirmations, or statements that affirm one's positive qualities or aspirations, can be another valuable tool for individuals with ADHD seeking to cultivate a more positive self-image and outlook on life. While it may initially feel awkward or insincere to recite affirmations, research suggests that regularly engaging in this practice can gradually rewire the brain, leading to increased self-confidence and self-esteem.

When crafting affirmations, it's essential to focus on strengths and areas of potential growth rather than dwelling on perceived shortcomings. For example, instead of saying, "I am not easily distracted," individuals can reframe it as, "I am capable of focusing my attention when needed." By framing affirmations in a positive and empowering way, individuals with ADHD can harness the power of their thoughts to propel them towards their goals.

Mindful reflection complements the practice of positive affirmations by deepening self-awareness and promoting self-compassion. Through mindfulness techniques such as meditation or mindful breathing, individuals can cultivate a non-judgmental awareness of their thoughts, emotions, and bodily sensations. This heightened awareness allows individuals to observe their inner experiences without becoming entangled in them, thereby reducing reactivity and enhancing emotional regulation.

By integrating positive affirmations with mindful reflection, individuals with ADHD can gradually cultivate a more compassionate and accepting relationship with themselves. Rather than being consumed by self-critical thoughts or negative self-talk, they can learn to acknowledge their challenges with kindness and optimism, recognizing that setbacks are a natural part of the human experience.

12.3 Mindfulness and Positive Psychology Interventions

Mindfulness, with its emphasis on present-moment awareness and non-judgmental acceptance, aligns closely with the principles of positive psychology. Both approaches share a common goal of promoting psychological well-being and resilience by fostering positive emotions, enhancing self-awareness, and cultivating meaningful connections with others.

Mindfulness-based interventions, such as mindfulness-based stress reduction (MBSR) or mindfulness-based cognitive therapy (MBCT), have been shown to be effective in reducing symptoms of ADHD and improving overall functioning. These interventions typically involve a combination of mindfulness practices, cognitive restructuring techniques, and psychoeducation aimed at empowering individuals to manage their symptoms more effectively.

In the context of positive psychology, mindfulness serves as a foundational practice for cultivating positive emotions such as gratitude, compassion, and joy. By bringing mindful awareness to everyday experiences, individuals can savor the simple pleasures of life and develop a greater appreciation for the richness of the present moment.

Integrating mindfulness with positive psychology interventions can create a synergistic effect, amplifying the benefits of both approaches. For example, combining gratitude practices with mindfulness meditation can deepen one's sense of appreciation for life's blessings while simultaneously enhancing emotional resilience and psychological well-being.

In summary, cultivating gratitude, practicing positive affirmations, and integrating mindfulness with principles of positive psychology offer valuable tools for individuals with ADHD seeking to enhance their overall well-being and resilience. By embracing a mindset of gratitude, fostering self-compassion through affirmations and mindful reflection, and incorporating mindfulness into daily life, individuals can cultivate a more positive outlook and navigate the challenges of ADHD with greater ease and resilience.

13

Mindfulness in Relapse Prevention

Chapter 13 explores the critical aspect of relapse prevention in managing ADHD symptoms through mindfulness-based strategies. Understanding the early warning signs of relapse, implementing mindfulness techniques to prevent relapse, and developing a structured relapse prevention plan are essential components for individuals seeking long-term management of ADHD.

13.1 Recognizing Early Warning Signs of ADHD Relapse

Recognizing the early warning signs of ADHD relapse is crucial for individuals to intervene before symptoms escalate. These signs may vary among individuals but often include:

1. Increased Impulsivity: Individuals may notice a return of impulsive behaviors, such as interrupting conversations or engaging in risky activities without considering consequences.

2. Difficulty Concentrating: A decline in focus and attention span may manifest as difficulty completing tasks, becoming easily distracted, or experiencing racing thoughts.

3. Emotional Dysregulation: Heightened emotional responses, such as irritability, mood swings, or feelings of overwhelm, may signal a relapse in ADHD symptoms.

4. Procrastination and Disorganization: Individuals may find it challenging to initiate tasks, manage time effectively, or maintain organization, leading to increased stress and frustration.

5. Decline in Self-Care Practices: Neglecting self-care activities, such as exercise, healthy eating, or adequate sleep, can indicate a regression in ADHD management.

Recognizing these early warning signs requires self-awareness and mindfulness. By staying present and attuned to their thoughts, emotions, and behaviors, individuals can detect subtle changes indicative of an impending relapse.

13.2 Preventing Relapse through Mindfulness-Based Strategies

Preventing relapse involves implementing mindfulness-based strategies to address emerging symptoms and maintain stability. Here are several mindfulness techniques that can be effective in preventing ADHD relapse:

1. Mindful Breathing: Practicing deep, diaphragmatic breathing can help individuals regulate emotions and reduce impulsivity.

Taking slow, deliberate breaths while focusing on the sensations of each inhale and exhale grounds individuals in the present moment, allowing them to respond thoughtfully rather than react impulsively.

2. Body Scan Meditation: Engaging in a body scan meditation involves systematically directing attention to different parts of the body, noticing any sensations without judgment. This practice promotes body awareness and relaxation, reducing stress and enhancing emotional regulation.

3. Mindful Movement: Incorporating mindful movement practices such as yoga, tai chi, or qigong can improve focus, balance, and overall well-being. Paying attention to the sensations of movement and breath fosters a mind-body connection, reducing impulsivity and increasing self-awareness.

4. Cognitive Defusion: Cognitive defusion techniques involve observing and distancing oneself from intrusive thoughts or negative self-talk. By recognizing thoughts as transient mental events rather than absolute truths, individuals can prevent them from triggering impulsive or emotional reactions.

5. Mindful Eating: Paying attention to the sensory experience of eating, including taste, texture, and aroma, promotes mindful eating habits. By slowing down and savoring each bite, individuals can reduce impulsivity around food choices and cultivate a healthier relationship with eating.

6. Self-Compassion Practice: Practicing self-compassion involves treating oneself with kindness and understanding, par-

ticularly during challenging times. By acknowledging the difficulties of managing ADHD and offering oneself support and encouragement, individuals can prevent negative self-judgment and reduce stress.

Implementing these mindfulness-based strategies requires consistency and commitment. Engaging in daily mindfulness practices builds resilience and equips individuals with the tools they need to navigate potential relapse triggers effectively.

13.3 Developing a Mindfulness-Based Relapse Prevention Plan

Developing a structured relapse prevention plan tailored to individual needs is essential for maintaining long-term ADHD management. This plan integrates mindfulness practices with specific strategies for recognizing and addressing relapse triggers. Here's a step-by-step approach to creating a mindfulness-based relapse prevention plan:

1. Identify Personal Triggers: Reflect on past experiences to identify situations, emotions, or behaviors that have preceded ADHD relapse episodes. Common triggers may include stress, lack of sleep, or certain environmental factors.

2. Establish Early Warning Signs: Based on identified triggers, define specific early warning signs that indicate a potential relapse. These signs serve as indicators to initiate proactive intervention before symptoms escalate.

3. Mindfulness-Based Coping Strategies: Compile a list of mindfulness techniques and coping strategies that have been effective

in managing ADHD symptoms in the past. Include both formal practices, such as meditation and yoga, and informal techniques, such as deep breathing exercises or mindful walking.

4. Create a Crisis Plan: Develop a crisis plan outlining steps to take in the event of an acute ADHD relapse. Include contact information for healthcare providers, support resources, and emergency hotlines, ensuring access to assistance when needed.

5. Daily Maintenance Plan: Establish a daily maintenance plan incorporating regular mindfulness practices, self-care activities, and healthy habits. Schedule time for meditation, exercise, adequate sleep, and nutritious meals to support overall well-being and resilience.

6. Review and Revision: Regularly review and revise the relapse prevention plan based on ongoing self-monitoring and feedback from support networks. Adjust strategies as needed to address changing circumstances and evolving needs.

By proactively implementing a mindfulness-based relapse prevention plan, individuals with ADHD can mitigate the risk of relapse and maintain stability in their daily lives. Consistent practice of mindfulness techniques equips individuals with the skills and resilience necessary to navigate challenges and sustain long-term well-being.

14

Integrating Mindfulness into Everyday Life

In the pursuit of a more mindful existence, Chapter 14 offers a roadmap for seamlessly embedding mindfulness into the tapestry of daily living. This chapter serves as a beacon, guiding individuals on how to transcend the boundaries of mere practice and embrace mindfulness as an inherent aspect of their lifestyle. From dismantling barriers hindering consistent engagement to infusing mindfulness into diverse life domains, this comprehensive exploration illuminates the path toward embodying mindfulness beyond formal sessions.

14.1 Making Mindfulness a Lifestyle Choice

To embark on the journey of making mindfulness a lifestyle choice, one must first undergo a paradigm shift—a shift from perceiving mindfulness as a sporadic activity to recognizing it as a fundamental pillar of holistic well-being. This entails introspection, a process wherein individuals delineate their motives behind integrating mindfulness into their lives. Whether driven by a desire to alleviate stress, heighten focus, or fortify relationships, clarifying these intentions lays a sturdy foundation for sustained commitment.

Setting realistic and tangible goals serves as the cornerstone for weaving mindfulness into the fabric of everyday life. Rather than striving for perfection or adhering to rigid schedules, the emphasis is on integrating mindfulness into daily routines in a manner that feels both attainable and sustainable. Commencing with brief, daily practices and gradually expanding them as comfort levels increase enables a gentle assimilation of mindfulness into one's lifestyle.

Consistency emerges as the linchpin in actualizing mindfulness as a lifestyle choice. Thus, individuals are encouraged to discern opportunities for embedding mindfulness into their existing habits and rituals. Whether it be infusing mindfulness into mundane activities such as brushing teeth, savoring meals, or commuting to work, the objective is to facilitate its seamless integration into the fabric of daily existence.

14.2 Overcoming Barriers to Consistent Practice

Invariably, the path to mindfulness is strewn with obstacles, necessitating a vigilant appraisal and mitigation of barriers hindering consistent engagement.

Among the common impediments, time constraints loom large in contemporary society. Amidst the hustle and bustle of daily life, carving out dedicated time for mindfulness may appear daunting. Yet, it is imperative to acknowledge that mindfulness need not monopolize extensive time slots. Even fleeting moments of focused awareness can yield profound benefits. Thus, individuals are encouraged to schedule periodic "mindfulness breaks" throughout their day, irrespective of their brevity.

Resistance or procrastination poses yet another formidable barrier to consistent mindfulness practice. Oftentimes, individuals recoil from engaging in mindfulness activities, driven by discomfort or aversion toward confronting their inner landscape. In such instances, cultivating an attitude of curiosity and openness towards mindfulness can circumvent the shackles of resistance, fostering a more receptive disposition.

External distractions, ranging from ambient noise to incessant interruptions, present yet another obstacle to sustained mindfulness practice. Creating an environment conducive to mindfulness, characterized by minimal distractions and fortified boundaries, fosters an optimal milieu for nurturing focus and concentration during practice sessions.

14.3 Cultivating Mindfulness in Work, Home, and Social Settings

Mindfulness transcends the confines of formal meditation, permeating diverse facets of existence, including work, home, and social interactions.

In the professional realm, mindfulness serves as a potent

catalyst for enhancing focus, productivity, and overall well-being. By incorporating simple mindfulness techniques such as conscious breathing or periodic mindfulness breaks, individuals can ameliorate stress levels and bolster cognitive acuity. Moreover, infusing mindfulness into collaborative endeavors or workplace interactions engenders a culture of enhanced communication and synergy.

Within the sanctum of home, mindfulness fosters deeper connections and harmony among family members. Practicing mindful communication and active listening engenders mutual understanding and empathy, thereby fortifying familial bonds. Furthermore, infusing mindfulness into routine household chores or daily rituals imbues them with a renewed sense of presence and appreciation.

In social settings, mindfulness augments the quality of interpersonal engagements, fostering authentic connections and rapport. By embodying attentive presence and genuine curiosity during interactions, individuals cultivate an environment conducive to heartfelt exchanges and mutual support. Furthermore, practicing compassion and non-judgment fosters empathy and inclusivity, nurturing a culture of warmth and acceptance.

In conclusion, integrating mindfulness into everyday life transcends the realm of mere practice, heralding a profound shift in consciousness. By cultivating mindfulness as a lifestyle choice, surmounting barriers to consistent engagement, and infusing mindfulness into diverse life domains, individuals embark on a transformative odyssey towards embodying mindfulness in its fullest essence.

15

Continuing Your Mindfulness Journey

15.1 Reflecting on Your Mindfulness Progress

Reflecting on your mindfulness progress is an essential step in your journey towards greater self-awareness and well-being. Take some time to pause and reflect on how mindfulness has impacted various aspects of your life since you began your practice. Start by considering the changes you've noticed in your thoughts, emotions, and behaviors. Have you become more aware of your thought patterns and emotional reactions? Are you able to respond to challenging situations with greater calm and clarity? Reflecting on these changes can help you appreciate the benefits of mindfulness and motivate you to continue your practice.

Next, consider the specific mindfulness techniques that have been most effective for you. Whether it's mindful breathing, body scan meditation, or mindful walking, identify the practices that resonate most with you and have contributed to your well-being. Reflect on how consistent you've been with your practice and any challenges you've encountered along the way. Acknowledge your progress and celebrate your successes, no matter how small they may seem.

In addition to reflecting on your personal progress, it can also be helpful to seek feedback from others. This could be from a mindfulness teacher, therapist, or trusted friend or family member who has observed changes in you since you began practicing mindfulness. Hearing about your progress from others can provide valuable insights and encouragement to continue your journey.

15.2 Advanced Mindfulness Techniques and Resources

As you continue your mindfulness journey, you may want to explore more advanced techniques to deepen your practice and further enhance your well-being. Here are some advanced mindfulness techniques you may consider:

1. Loving-Kindness Meditation: This practice involves cultivating feelings of love, compassion, and goodwill towards yourself and others. It can help cultivate a sense of connection and empathy, which can be particularly beneficial for individuals with ADHD who may struggle with impulsivity and interpersonal relationships.

2. Open Monitoring Meditation: Also known as choiceless awareness, this practice involves observing your thoughts, emotions, and sensations without judgment or attachment. It

can help develop a greater sense of spacious awareness and acceptance of whatever arises in the present moment.

3. Mindful Movement Practices: Incorporating movement into your mindfulness practice can help cultivate embodied awareness and release tension in the body. Practices such as yoga, tai chi, and qigong can be particularly beneficial for individuals with ADHD, as they combine physical movement with mindful attention to breath and body sensations.

4. Mindful Eating: This practice involves bringing awareness to the experience of eating, including the taste, texture, and smell of food, as well as the sensations of hunger and fullness. It can help cultivate a healthier relationship with food and prevent impulsive eating behaviors often associated with ADHD.

In addition to these advanced techniques, there are many resources available to support your ongoing mindfulness practice. This may include books, online courses, workshops, retreats, and mindfulness apps. Consider exploring different resources to find what resonates with you and supports your continued growth and development.

15.3 Sustaining Mindfulness Practice for Long-Term Benefits

Sustaining a mindfulness practice over the long term requires commitment, consistency, and patience. Here are some tips to help you maintain your practice and reap the long-term benefits of mindfulness:

1. Establish a Routine: Set aside dedicated time each day for

mindfulness practice, whether it's first thing in the morning, during your lunch break, or before bed. Consistency is key to developing a habit, so try to practice at the same time and place each day.

2. Start Small: If you're new to mindfulness or struggling to maintain a consistent practice, start with just a few minutes of meditation each day and gradually increase the duration as you build your capacity for mindfulness.

3. Find Support: Surround yourself with a supportive community of fellow practitioners who can provide encouragement, accountability, and inspiration. This may include joining a mindfulness group or attending regular meditation sessions at a local center.

4. Be Kind to Yourself: Remember that mindfulness is a practice, not a perfect. Be gentle with yourself and approach your practice with an attitude of curiosity, openness, and self-compassion. Accept that there will be ups and downs along the way, and that's all part of the journey.

5. Stay Curious: Approach your mindfulness practice with a sense of curiosity and exploration, rather than trying to achieve a specific outcome. Be open to whatever arises in the present moment and trust that your practice will unfold naturally over time.

15.4 Conclusion

Continuing your mindfulness journey is a lifelong process of self-discovery, growth, and transformation. By reflecting on your progress, exploring advanced techniques, and sustaining your practice over the long term, you can cultivate greater awareness, resilience, and well-being in your life. Remember that mindfulness is not a quick fix or cure-all, but rather a way of being that can enrich every aspect of your life. Stay committed to your practice, be patient with yourself, and trust in the power of mindfulness to support you on your journey towards greater peace, clarity, and fulfillment.